Hohokam Indians of the Tucson Basin

by
Linda M. Gregonis
and
Karl J. Reinhard

THE UNIVERSITY OF ARIZONA PRESS

TUCSON, ARIZONA

About the Authors

LINDA M. GREGONIS, a staff archaeologist with the Colorado State Historic Preservation Office, supervised the excavation of the Hardy Site at Fort Lowell Park. She holds a B.A. and M.A. in anthropology from the University of Arizona and has done archaeological work, including research, writing, survey, and excavation, for the Bureau of Land Management Denver Service Center and the Cultural Resource Management Section of the Arizona State Museum.

KARL J. REINHARD has done archaeological work, including excavation, survey, and laboratory analysis, at Salmon Ruins in New Mexico and in several areas in Arizona. He assisted in directing the excavation of the Hardy Site and has specialized in ceramic analysis. He holds a B.A. in anthropology from the University of Arizona and in 1982 was continuing advanced studies at Northern Arizona University.

Photos in this volume are used by permission of the Arizona State Museum, University of Arizona, and all but the one on page 7 were taken by Helga Teiwes.

Second Printing 1983
THE UNIVERSITY OF ARIZONA PRESS
Copyright © 1979
The Arizona Board of Regents
All Rights Reserved
Manufactured in the U.S.A.

Library of Congress Cataloging in Publication Data

Gregonis, Linda M
 The Hohokam Indians of the Tucson Basin.

 Bibliography: p.
 1. Hohokam culture. 2. Indians of North America
—Arizona—Tucson region—Antiquities. 3. Hardy site,
Ariz. 4. Tucson region, Ariz.—Antiquities.
5. Arizona—Antiquities. I. Reinhard, Karl J.,
joint author. II. Arizona. State Museum, Tucson.
III. Title
E99.H68G73   979.1′77   79-20097
ISBN 0-8165-0700-7

Contents

Preserving Archaeological Sites

Archaeological remains, both prehistoric and historic, are presently being threatened by the rapid expansion of modern cities. Tucson is just one of many cities in the Southwest that is destroying traces of its past by building on prehistoric and historic sites. The construction cannot always be stopped, but some of the archaeological remains might be saved. If you know of an historic or prehistoric site that is in danger of destruction, please inform your local university, museum, or historical or archaeological society.

Foreword

Until the spring of 1979, visitors to Tucson and the city's residents had little opportunity to learn about the "earliest Tucsonans"—the prehistoric Hohokam—even though much of the Tucson area had been occupied for many centuries by the Hohokam. This booklet and an exhibit at Fort Lowell Park in Tucson have been prepared to help interpret the lifeway of these early desert people.

The Arizona State Museum and the Department of Anthropology at the University of Arizona had conducted archaeological research in the Tucson Basin—that area encompassed by the mountains around the city of Tucson—for many years. However, no special effort was made to inform the public about the Hohokam. In 1975, a concerned amateur archaeologist called the museum to report that Hohokam pottery and tools had been exposed during construction at Fort Lowell Park, a Pima County park in the northeast part of the city. Archaeologists at the museum were aware that a large Hohokam village had once existed along Rillito Creek in the vicinity of the park, and that installation of park facilities on several occasions had unearthed prehistoric remains. The new area reported was unique, however, because it had been private property and had only recently been purchased by the Pima County Parks and Recreation Department for expansion of Fort Lowell Park. A reconnaissance of the property showed that several zones contained deep, undisturbed deposits of Hohokam material. This large Hohokam village was designated as the Hardy Site.

When it was learned that this area would be developed eventually by the county for public use, the concept emerged of an interpretive exhibit in the park on the Tucson Basin Hohokam. This seemed appropriate, as the park already contained an interpretive unit on the military establishment of Fort Lowell in the late nineteenth century. This military use and the Hohokam occupation, which extended back to at least A.D. 500, made this location one of the oldest and longest occupied areas in Tucson.

The Arizona State Museum assumed responsibility for developing this concept and, from the beginning, received strong support and assistance from Pima County Parks and Recreation. A planning grant from the National Endowment for the Humanities enabled museum staff to carry out background research for the exhibit, and a subsequent implementation grant from NEH provided for additional research, development of a display in the Fort Lowell Museum, installation of an outdoor exhibit, and preparation of this booklet. The outdoor exhibit required excavation of a portion of the Hardy Site, and this work was conducted over a two-year period on weekends by students from the Department of Anthropology at the University of Arizona, and by a number of dedicated local amateur archaeologists.

When the exhibit opened in April, 1979, a number of important things had been accomplished. Interpretive panels installed at the site and artifacts displayed at the Fort Lowell Museum provided an opportunity for the public to learn how the Hohokam adapted to and made a living in the Tucson desert environment more than a thousand years ago. The panels and display also illustrated the many ways in which the Hohokam artistically enriched their lives. Public involvement in the preservation of Arizona's cultural heritage has also been achieved. Throughout the period of excavation, anyone who wished to observe or participate in the archaeological work was encouraged to do so. This experience helped many to understand the need for conserving archaeological sites and the importance of careful excavation and analysis. Finally, work at the site provided valuable training for a number of students and produced important new information on the Tucson Basin Hohokam. A final technical report on the results of the excavation is currently in preparation.

When plans were being developed for the public interpretive exhibit on the Tucson Basin Hohokam, it became apparent that, in addition to the outdoor exhibit panels and the display at the Fort Lowell Museum, a good synthesis of the Tucson Basin Hohokam was necessary for a more complete understanding of these people. This booklet has been prepared to fill the need for a layman's guide to the Hohokam archaeology of the Tucson Basin area. It is designed to provide basic information on the Hohokam and, at the same time, make these past desert dwellers more "real" by recreating as accurately as possible much of the daily routine of their lives. The booklet is best used in conjunction with visits to the outdoor exhibit at Fort Lowell Park, the Fort Lowell Museum, and the Arizona State Museum. The outdoor exhibit provides a certain "feel" for the natural environment and lifeway of the Hohokam; the Fort Lowell Museum contains artifactual materials, recovered from excavations at the Hardy Site; and the Arizona State Museum has a series of exhibits that portray the Hohokam culture as a major lifeway of the southern Arizona desert.

As project director, I have had the pleasure of working with a great many dedicated people in helping to interpret the prehistory of the Tucson Basin Hohokam. Linda Gregonis, Karl Reinhard, the staffs of the Pima County Parks and Recreation Department and the Arizona State Museum, many students, and others, all share in the success of our goal to bring the Tucson Basin Hohokam to life.

R. Gwinn Vivian
Associate Director
Arizona State Museum

Acknowledgments

We would like to thank the many people who have been involved in the Tucson Basin Hohokam Interpretive Project. First, we are grateful to the students and other volunteers, especially Clare Vynalek, who participated in the excavation of the Hardy Site, and to Gene Laos, Gale Bundrick, and the Pima County Parks and Recreation Commission for allowing us to excavate and encouraging us to interpret the site. We appreciate the help of those who participated in the planning and development of exhibits at the park: Ernie Leavitt, Art Brownlee, Rocky Brittain, Todd Ruttenbeck, George Chambers, Michael Lord, Dave Faust, Jeanne Jones, Debra Meier and members of the Young Adult Conservation Corps. We would also like to thank Debra and Jeanne, as well as Chris Smith, for their illustrations in this booklet. Special thanks are due to Helga Teiwes for her photographic work and to Sue Ruiz for typing drafts of the manuscript. We appreciate the insightful comments given by those who read the initial drafts of this work. We thank Professor Emil Haury, whose work in the Hohokam area enabled us to write many portions of this booklet. We would especially like to thank Gwinn Vivian and Donald Sayner, without whom this project could never have been started or finished. Gwinn Vivian, as project director, aided in the development of all aspects of the project and encouraged us in its completion. Donald Sayner's illustrating expertise was constantly used by us, and we appreciate his enthusiasm and patience throughout. Last, we would like to acknowledge with thanks the support of the National Endowment for the Humanities for this project and, in particular, cite the help of Ms. Suzanne Schell during all phases of the work. Appreciation is also due the University of Arizona Press for bringing about publication.

LMG and KJR

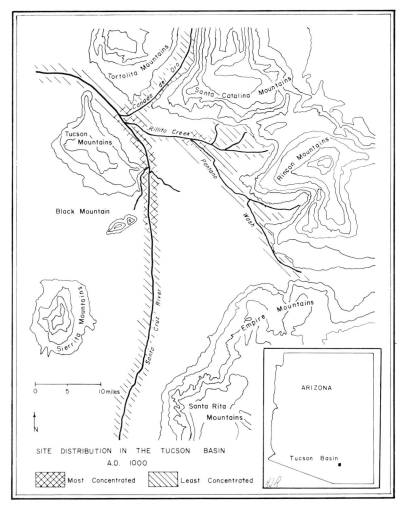

SITE DISTRIBUTION IN THE TUCSON BASIN
A.D. 1000

Most Concentrated   Least Concentrated

By A.D. 1000, the Hohokam were using all parts of the Tucson Basin. They built their villages along streams and rivers and hunted and gathered in the foothills and mountains.

The Hohokam World

Centuries before Europeans first saw the Tucson Basin, a group of Indians with a distinctive way of life had settled there. Known today as the Hohokam (hō-hō-kăm), these people built villages close to streams in order to farm the region's rich bottomlands. They lived in the basin from about A.D. 300 to 1500. The Tucson Basin villagers were part of the larger Hohokam world, whose inhabitants lived in the Sonoran Desert of southern Arizona. They ably adapted themselves to the desert environment by farming along drainages and hunting and gathering in the desert and mountains.

Predecessors of the Hohokam

The Hohokam were not the first to live in the Tucson Basin. During the Ice Age, people migrated from Siberia across the Bering Strait into Alaska. These "Paleo-Indians" followed herds of big game into North America. By 9500 B.C., bands of hunters wandered into southern Arizona, where they found a desert grassland. Mammoths that thrived in the grassland were hunted by the Indians. Hunters trapped mammoths along streams and lakes and killed them with spears. The carcasses of the ponderous beasts were butchered on the spot and the meat was cooked nearby. Although best known for their mammoth hunting, the Paleo-Indians ate other types of animals including bison. They also collected and ate plant foods.

As the climate warmed and dried after the end of the Ice Age, mammoths and associated animals such as horses and camels began to disappear from North America. To the Indians, the change was gradual. They found fewer mammoths each year, so they supplemented their diet with a variety of plant foods and smaller game.

Groups of Indians discovered the nutritive value of weed and grass seeds, ground to flour on flat rocks and made into gruels and breads. The use of grinding slabs marks the beginning of the Desert Archaic tradition. In the Tucson area, the Desert Archaic tradition lasted from 7000 B.C. to about A.D. 300. During that time, small bands of people moved around the basin gathering plants. They lived primarily in the open, but probably also built temporary shelters. Summer found them in the foothills, collecting foods such as cactus fruits and mesquite beans. Acorns, pine nuts, and other foods from the higher mountains were gathered in the fall. Although hunting took place the year-round it was especially important in the winter and spring months when plant foods were scarce. The Archaic people established camps at each collection point, to which they returned year after year.

Late in the Archaic Period, corn was introduced into the region from Mexico. People planted the crop near camps with permanent water sources. After planting, the hunter-gatherers moved on to gather wild foods, returning only to harvest the ripened crop. They treated the cultivated food as one more native plant to be gathered.

The Hohokam

About 300 B.C., the Hohokam, an agricultural group, migrated from Mexico into southern Arizona and settled in villages along the Salt and Gila rivers. As their population grew, they began settling areas around the Gila-Salt heartland. At about A.D. 200, a few Hohokam families apparently moved to the Tucson Basin and built their homes along the Santa Cruz and Rillito rivers. These early villagers introduced a new lifeway into the area.

The Archaic people, living in small scattered camps in the basin, gradually absorbed the new lifeway. The adopted the Hohokam "rancheria" style of living, where people occupied widely separated house groups within a village. They began making pottery and digging ditches to water the newly arrived Hohokam varieties of corn, beans, squash, and cotton. These Tucson Basin Hohokam were soon trading for seashells, copying from the Hohokam heartland, and using such typical goods as carved stone bowls and clay human figurines. However, they also retained, in part, the seasonal hunting and gathering of their Archaic predecessors. About half of their food was cultivated in fields, and the rest was collected by villagers who maintained seasonal camps in the mountains and foothills.

2

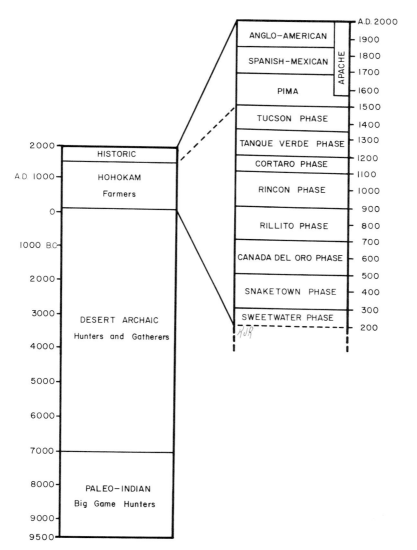

The Tucson Basin has a long human history. The Hohokam occupation of the basin has been divided into several phases on the basis of changes in pottery types and architecture.

After A.D. 1100, influence from the heartland Hohokam began to dwindle, and cultural ties were strengthened with the Mogollon people to the north and east, resulting in a blend of Hohokam and Mogollon traits in the Tucson Basin. Around A.D. 1250, villagers began building adobe-walled houses, and Hohokam potters innovated new designs and created a pottery style that was widely copied by groups around the Tucson Basin. By 1350, some people had moved into a few large communities composed of abovegound, apartment-like dwellings, but the population as a whole seems to have declined. The reasons for these cultural changes are not clear, but environmental deterioration (perhaps including droughts) and changes in social organization brought about by the collapse of major cultures in Mesoamerica have both been suggested as possible causes.

By 1500, the Tucson Basin Indians had returned to living in scattered, Hohokam-like rancherías. These people, known today as the Pimas and Papagos, were encountered by the Spanish in the 1600s, when they first entered the Tucson Basin.

The Tucson Basin Indians were a small part of the total Hohokam occupation of southern Arizona. This occupation extended from Gila Bend on the west to Globe on the east, and from the north near Flagstaff to near the Arizona-Mexico border in the south. The Gila and Salt River valleys remained the heartland of the Hohokam culture through time. As in the Tucson Basin, the culture of the Hohokam in areas outside the heartland varied in small ways. However, each had in common a sedentary lifestyle, a dependence on agriculture, and a unique ceremonial and trading system.

The Tucson Basin

The lifeway of the Tucson Basin Hohokam was molded by the local environment as the Indians took advantage of the area's rich natural setting. The Tucson Basin lies near the eastern edge of the Basin and Range Province of the Sonoran Desert. This area is characterized by low, discontinuous mountain ranges jutting up from the flat desert plain. The narrow mountain ranges are widely spaced and generally run north to south. Between the mountains are areas where sediment has collected from eroding mountain slopes to form shallow basins. Intermittent rivers flow along the basin floors.

The Tucson Basin is enclosed by five mountains ranges. The Tucsons and Sierritas form the western and southern boundaries, and the Santa

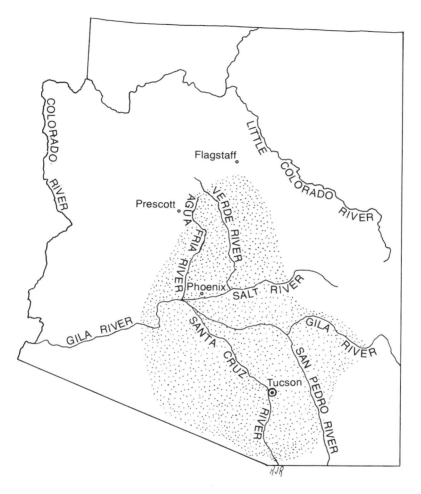

The extent of Hohokam occupation in Arizona is shown by the shaded area on this map.

Catalina, Rincon, and Santa Rita mountains make up the northern, eastern, and southern boundaries. The Tucsons and Sierritas are typical low Basin and Range Province mountains, formed by volcanism and the fracturing of the earth's surface layers. The Catalinas, Rincons, and Santa Ritas, however, are high, massive, eroded remnants of underground intrusions of grantic rock. Their pine-covered summits receive twenty to twenty-five inches of rainfall annually, three times the average for the Sonoran Desert. Rainfall in the Tucson Basin is also high in comparison to the major portion of the desert—eleven inches annually in contrast to seven. Before the expansion of Tucson and the overuse of ground water, the precipitation maintained a high water table and a healthy natural environment.

Prehistorically, parts of the basin looked quite different than they do today. By destroying plant cover on the slopes, overgrazing and construction in modern times have damaged some of the foothill areas. Instead of being trapped by vegetation and sinking into the ground, rainwater now tends to run down the hills, contributing to arroyo-cutting and causing flooding.

Although now the local streams flow only occasionally and are entrenched in deep channels, this has not always been the case. As recently as the late 1800s, the streams flowed on the surface and, by means of ditches, provided water to irrigate crops grown in the floodplain. Reports of the Tucson Basin written between A.D. 1700 and 1870 mention that the rivers flowed year-round, that cottonwood and mesquite grew along their banks, and that, in some places, beavers built their dams.

Even today, the Tucson Basin is rich in plant and animal life. The variety of plants ranges from desert grasses and scrub trees to piñon and ponderosa pine forests on the mountain sides, and from cacti on the desert floor to cottonwood and willow along the streams. The varied vegetation supports an equally varied animal life, from desert reptiles and rodents to deer and mountain sheep.

The Sonoran Desert is easily farmed when water is available. Precipitation comes in two distinct wet seasons, late winter and midsummer, providing good conditions for agriculture. Another factor making the desert suitable for farming is a long growing season, about 250 days. Up to the late 1800s, the permanently flowing streams provided enough water for canal irrigation. At present, by pumping underground water, many crops can still be grown in the desert.

A variety of useful plants available to the Hohokam can be found on the desert floor and lower slopes of the mountains. In the foreground are prickly pear and barrel cactus. The large, tree-like cactus on the left is a saguaro. To the right of the saguaro are palo verde trees and cholla cactus.

In large part, the topography and environment of the Tucson Basin determined where and how the Hohokam lived. Villages were built next to the permanent streams and springs that ringed the basin, and villagers ventured into the dry center of the basin only on hunting and collecting expeditions. Where saguaro and mesquite groves grew the thickest, the Hohokam established camps that they returned to each year to harvest fruits and seeds. The diversity of topography and natural resources in the Tucson Basin allowed the Indians efficiently to combine hunting and gathering with agriculture and a sedentary lifestyle.

The Hohokam Lifeway

To reconstruct the lifeway of the Hohokam, different kinds of information were used. Knowledge of architectural features and material remains came from excavations of villages in the Tucson Basin and elsewhere in the Hohokam area. Professor Emil Haury, longtime researcher in Hohokam archaeology, provided insights into the use of objects and features found at those sites. To reconstruct the Hohokam's daily activities and social structure, ethnographic accounts of the Pima and Papago cultures were used. The Pimas and Papagos are believed to be descendents of the Hohokam and historically shared a similar lifestyle with their predecessors. Finally, the fragments of information were bound together by our imaginations to recreate the lifeway of the Tucson Basin Hohokam.

Agriculture

Hohokam villagers grew cotton and corn, as well as several types of beans and squash. In the Gila and Salt River valleys, the Indians built a complex system of canals, to lead water from the rivers to their fields above the floodplain. In contrast, the Tucson Basin people practiced floodwater farming; that is, they planted crops in the floodplains of the rivers which flooded their banks after major storms. The rivers at that time were shallow, meandering streams; they were not deeply entrenched as they are now. The Indians probably also dug short irrigation ditches, to direct water to crops grown on the floodplain. In parts of the basin where floodplains were not available, the Hohokam farmed at the mouths of arroyos. They also built rock terraces and check dams

8

on hill slopes and in washes to catch rainfall runoff. The Indian's only agricultural tools were sharp, wooden digging sticks and handheld hoes made from thin rock slabs. They may also have used broken pieces of pottery as hand shovels.

Like other North American Indians, the Hohokam probably planted their crops in a series of small earth mounds. Corn, beans, squash, and cotton could all be planted in the same mound, so that each plant provided the others with nutrients and weed protection. Planted in March after the last winter frost, crops were ready to be harvested in July. Villagers prepared much of their harvest for use during winter and spring.

Corn was a mainstay in the Hohokam diet. Although the Indians roasted and ate corn on the cob during harvest season, they dried and ground most of the corn into flour before use. The villagers may have made corn flour into dumplings and bread, thickened stews with it, or dropped a handful into a jar of water to make a nourishing drink.

The Hohokam ground the kernels of corn with stone tools called *manos* and *metates*. The Indians made metates from large rocks. They shaped the rocks into thick slabs or troughs, with a slightly roughened grinding surface that held kernels of corn in place during grinding. The mano, which was held in the hand, was made from a smaller stone, also slightly roughened. In using the tools, the Indians ground the rough surfaces down; consequently, they ate small bits of rock with every meal. As a result, the teeth of most adult Hohokam were worn smooth.

Other staples in the Hohokam diet were beans and squash. Dried or parched after shelling, beans were added to stews or boiled by themselves. Squash could have been used in several ways—the blossoms boiled, the seeds parched, or strips of the fruit dried for use in winter.

Cotton was used for both food and clothing. Seeds of the plant were parched, ground, and formed into cakes. Cotton fiber was spun into yarn and then woven into ponchos, shirts, and belts. Finished clothing and bundles of yarn may have been traded by the Hohokam to other Indians in the Southwest.

In addition to cultivated plants, the Hohokam harvested weeds that grew in their fields. Among the weeds gathered for greens and seeds were pigweed, sunflower, and tansy mustard.

Hunting and Gathering

The Tucson Basin Hohokam constantly supplemented their agricultural diet with native foods. In drought years, the Indians depended heavily on wild plants and animals. The Hohokam collected mesquite beans from the trees that grew along the river banks. Villagers stored the bean pods in baskets and jars or mashed them into flour, using a mortar and pestle. This important resource could have been made into broths, stews, and breads.

The villagers also collected foods in the desert foothills, as do the Pimas and Papagos today. In June, July, and August, they gathered fruits of the saguaro, cholla, prickly pear, and barrel cactus. When collecting cactus fruits then, as now, groups of people camped in the cactus groves. They ate, dried, and cooked the plants at the camps. The Hohokam probably prepared cactus in much the same way as the Pimas and Papagos do. After removing the needles, cholla buds and prickly pear pads were baked slowly in pits. Cholla buds were also boiled. The Hohokam cooked down saguaro fruit into syrup and made cakes from the dried seed. The Indians probably made wine from the syrup. Other cactus fruits that were not eaten raw were dried and stored. The Indians returned to their villages only with those products that were to be saved for later use.

The Hohokam went on gathering expeditions to the mountains. There, they harvested agave crowns, acorns, manzanita berries, and other small fruits. The Indians roasted the agave crowns in pits to make a succulent meal. Berries and acorns collected in the mountains may have been used later as additives in otherwise bland stews and breads.

The Hohokam supplemented their primarily plant-food diet with meat. They had no domestic animals except the dog, so most meat was obtained by hunting. Deer and rabbit were the most important meat sources, but the Indians also killed and ate mountain sheep, antelope, and rodents, including mice and ground squirrels. Dove, quail, duck, and geese were among the birds hunted, and Indians who lived along larger rivers also ate fish. Not particular in their culinary habits, the Hohokam also added tortoises, lizards, and snakes to their diet.

Villagers hunted larger animals with bows and arrows. Birds, mice, lizards, and snakes could have been trapped or shot with arrows. During certain seasons, Indians conducted communal rabbit hunts. They drove rabbits and other small animals into nets strung across drainages.

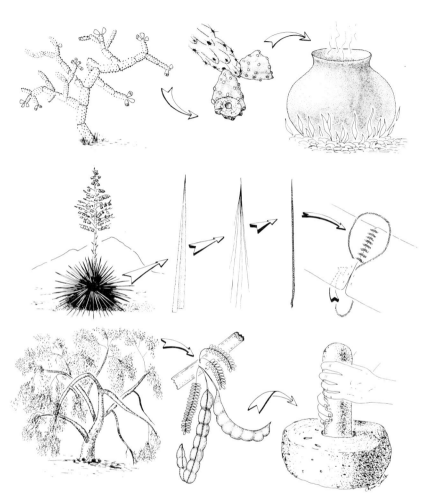

These are three of the many desert plants used by the Hohokam. At the top is a cholla cactus, the buds and fruits of which are boiled. In the center is a yucca, a plant of many uses. Indians sometimes made the leaves into thread by baring and twisting the plant's long fibers. The pointed end of each leaf was left at the end of the fiber to serve as a needle. Beans of the mesquite tree (bottom drawing) were an important part of the Hohokam diet. Ground with a mortar and pestle, mesquite bean flour could be used in broths, stews and breads.

Groups of people, walking slowly in a line towards the net, beat the bushes and shouted, to crowd the animals before them. Such a drive could have yielded enough food for a whole village during the late winter starvation time, when little of the stored plant foods remained.

Preparation of an animal for eating depended on the size and type of creature killed. Small animals, such as lizards, mice, and ground squirrels, could be eaten raw or could be spitted and cooked without gutting. The Indians skinned and gutted larger animals at the site of the kill, using sharp flakes of rock as knives. In a few seconds, the sharp fragments were knocked from a larger rock and were ready to use. When one flake became dull, it was discarded and another was made. After returning to the village, meat was portioned for roasting by using heavy stone choppers to cut joints and tendons. The meat could also be cut into strips with knife-like flakes and dried in the sun.

Native plants and animals were not used solely for food by the Hohokam. Materials for houses, ramadas, clothing, containers, ritual paraphernalia, and tools also came from the rivers, deserts, and mountains. The Hohokam were completely dependent on their immediate environment for all the necessities of life.

Dress

The Indians made simple clothing from animal skins and plant fibers. Villagers wore breechcloths and aprons. In winter, they wore buckskin shirts, cloth ponchos, and blankets. For foot protection, sandals were worn. On festive occasions they donned headdresses, turbans, head bands, belts and kilts.

The Hohokam made cordage (yarn) from cotton, milkweed, yucca, and agave fiber for weaving and sewing. To use yucca and agave, the Indians cut the leaves with a thin, saw-like stone blade. Then, using a heavy rock scraper, they stripped the flesh from the leaves, baring the fiber. Masses of fiber were twisted on a spindle whorl or rolled between hand and thigh to create long strings. Cordage was woven into fabric on looms or braided by hand and sewn. Villagers integrated color and design into the resulting fabrics by varying the weave, painting, or dyeing the cordage.

For needles, the villagers used the spike ends of yucca and agave leaves, leaving the attached stringy fiber as thread. Or, they fabricated needles from bone slivers or the long needles of barrel cactus. They also used bone awls in weaving and leather working.

A Hohokam rabbit hunt.

Animal skins were made into clothing. Tanned deerskins made fine shirts and sandals. To use rabbit and other small animal furs, Indians cut the prepared skins into narrow strips and attached the strips end-to-end. Then, using one or two of the long strings of fur, they twined the strips around a plant-fiber cordage base. The fur and cordage strings were then made into blankets. Woolen clothing was unknown in the Southwest until the 1600s, when the Spanish brought domestic sheep into the region.

The Hohokam also adorned themselves with jewelry. They wore bracelets, rings, earrings, necklaces, and nose plugs. Jewelry was made from seashells, semi-precious stones, pieces of pottery, and bone. The Hohokam probably painted themselves as well.

Jewelry worn by Hohokam men and women included items made from stone. At the top left is a mica pendant and below it are two turquoise beads and an argillite nose plug. In the center are turquoise pendants and pieces of inlay. At bottom right is a green serpentine bead.

Craft Production

Villagers made pottery by mixing clay, found in deposits along arroyos, with sand collected in washes. To prepare the clay, potters first ground it on metates. Then it was moistened and set aside to age for a few days. Next, the sand was sifted through basketry sifters to remove unwanted particles. Finally, potters mixed the sand and clay with water, to form a workable substance.

A potter formed each vessel from a molded clay base by adding coil upon coil of clay. She smoothed the coils together and shaped the pot with the use of a wooden paddle and stone tool called an anvil. After shaping the vessel, the potter may have decorated it with red paint made from crushed iron pigments. Iron pigments, such as hematite and limonite, could be found in local deposits or were obtained through trade. The designs were painted on pots with brushes made from yucca leaves or grass stems. Many pots were left unpainted.

Designs and decorative styles changed subtly through time, but decoration of Hohokam pottery was usually free-flowing and dynamic. Hatchured drawings of snakes, chevrons, and scrolls, as well as negative designs of lizards and other animals, characterized early pottery in the Tucson area. Other designs were added to these early types. Interlocking scrolls, triangles, zigzag and squiggly lines, circles, and frets were combined on vessels in hundreds of different ways. The final outcome of the decoration depended on the potter's ability to visualize a combination of designs and apply them to a vessel.

All Hohokam pottery was baked in open, wood fires. The Indians did not have kilns. Because of the uneven temperatures of an open fire, pottery was sometimes unintentionally blackened or overheated in places. The most skilled potters could either avoid the blackening and burning or were able to turn the resulting marks on the vessels into patterns. Sometimes vessels were intentionally blackened or smudged, usually on the interior of bowls. After firing, Tucson Basin pottery was usually brown or had red designs on a light brown to black background.

Pottery had many uses. In addition to making pots for cooking, serving, and storage, the Hohokam made ladles, scoops, figurines, and spindle whorls. Even after a pot broke, its pieces were still useful. Gaming pieces, pottery scrapers, scoops, and ornaments were some of the items made from broken pottery.

Hohokam potters painted many different designs on their pottery.

When lightweight, durable vessels were needed, the Hohokam made baskets. Villagers collected the fibrous leaves of yucca, cattail, and beargrass to weave into various shapes. Parts of the long, black, seed pods of Devil's Claw were woven into the baskets as decoration.

In preparation for weaving, the leaves and seed pods were soaked in water and repeatedly split to form thin strips. A weaver then coiled strips around each other, stitching the coils together with a separate leaf strip. The Hohokam also made plaited baskets by weaving flat strips of material over and under one another to form a pattern. These plaited baskets were more flexible but less durable than coiled baskets. Wicker baskets were rarely made by the Hohokam.

The resulting containers, in various shapes, served many purposes. Cooks used basket trays to parch corn and prepare foods. Coiled jars and plaited bags were used for gathering and storing foods. Loosely woven pieces were used for sifting corn meal and other materials. The Indians also made plaited sleeping mats.

Baskets similar to these were made by the Hohokam.

Perhaps one or two people in a village were trained in jewelry making, and skilled workers probably traded their products with other villages. Some craftsmen made ornaments from shells. Bracelets were made from large bivalve shells. The worker ground the top of each shell on a piece of sandstone until a small hole was worn. Then, using a chisel-like instrument, the hole was slowly enlarged to the desired size. Finally, the artisan used a stone reamer, a cylindrical object with a groove around one end, to smooth the inside of the bracelet. Bracelets were often carved and sometimes painted. Rings were made in a similar manner.

Indians created necklaces and earrings from shell beads and pendants. Sometimes, to make a bead or pendant, a craftsman simply drilled a hole through a whole shell. Other pieces were more elaborate. Pendants made from assorted fragments of shell were carved into triangles, discs, circles, and life forms such as frogs, birds, and horned toads. The Hohokam often drilled holes in broken bracelets and used them as pendants.

Craftsmen made delicate, disc-shaped beads by drilling a hole through a piece of shell with a cactus needle and using sand as an abrasive. Then the bead was roughly shaped by chipping. After assembling a string of the rough beads, the craftsman rolled the string on a grooved stone until the desired size was obtained. Beads and pendants were then strung together in whatever pattern suited the maker or wearer.

Hohokam craftsmen discovered how to decorate shell by etching. They were the only culture in the Americas to use the process, and they developed it several centuries before Europeans began to etch objects. To etch shell, the artisan put pitch or lac on a shell in a desired design. Then the shell was dipped into a weak acid made from fermented cactus juice. When the shell was removed from the acid, the uncovered portions were slightly eaten away, leaving the pitch-covered portion in relief. After removing the pitch, artisans sometimes painted the raised portions of the shell.

The Hohokam also made jewelry from minerals such as turquoise, steatite, argillite, and mica. The stones were worked in much the same way as shell. Artisans also carved incense burners, slate palettes, and other special items from other types of stone. Craftsmen may have specialized in making arrowheads, manos, and metates.

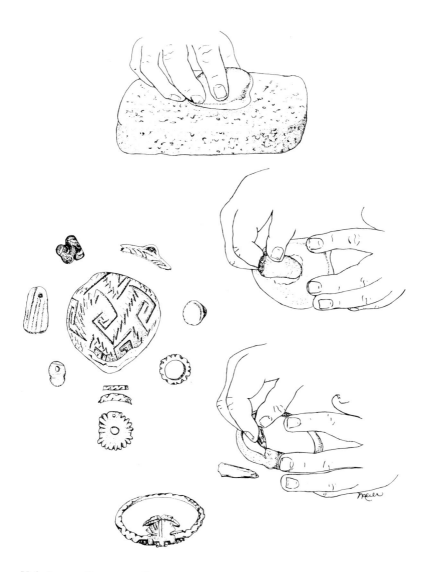

Hohokam craftsmen excelled in making shell jewelry. Shown here is the process of making a shell bracelet. The design on the whole shell in the center left was made by etching. Surrounding the etched shell are beads and pendants.

House Building

To shelter themselves, the Hohokam built simple brush- and dirt-covered pit houses. Building a pit house was a major task. Each house consisted of one rectangular, square, or oval room, with an entryway extending from one of the house's long walls. Shape and size of the pit house depended on the preferences and space needs of the builders.

To build a house, Indians first dug a pit, one to two feet deep. The pit allowed the house to stay cool in summer and warm in winter. Digging the pit for the house was a chore in the hard caliche soil of the Tucson Basin, because the Hohokam had only digging sticks, sherd scoops, and baskets with which to loosen and remove the earth.

Next, the pit house framework was built. The Indians dug postholes in several places inside the house and placed heavy mesquite or pine posts in them to support the roof. They dug a row of postholes around the house to support a framework for the outer walls. Cottonwood and willow posts may have been used for this framework. They then built

This cutaway drawing of a Hohokam pit house shows the different materials used in its construction. The inner support posts are covered with brush, and the brush is plastered over with mud and dirt. The small feature near the entryway is the clay-lined hearth.

20

the roof by placing beams across the major supports. Beams were covered by a network of saguaro and ocotillo ribs, and the whole roof was covered with brush.

The walls were also covered with brush or bundles of arrow weed and reeds. Finally, builders covered the whole structure with mud plaster and dirt. This type of brush and dirt covering is called wattle and daub. The outside of the completed structure looked like a small earthen mound, with an extension for the entryway, and blended well with the surrounding countryside.

In the interior, a smooth floor of mud plaster was laid. A small, circular, clay, fire hearth was built into the floor just inside the entryway. Sometimes a storage pit was dug into the floor. The pit was not lined with plaster, as the hard caliche soil made it almost impervious to water.

House furnishings were sparse. People slept on woven mats, laid directly on the floor, or on low sleeping platforms. Cooking and eating pots, large storage baskets, awls, arrows, and grinding tools were kept on the floor or on a platform, and light objects, such as baskets, were hung from walls and posts. Storage pots and various tools stood along house walls.

Village Organization

Houses were used for sleeping, storage, and protection during bad weather. The Hohokam spent most of their time out-of-doors, tending to their crops, collecting native plants, and hunting. They manufactured and repaired tools, and prepared and cooked food, in the shade provided by ramadas. Built of sturdy posts and covered with saguaro ribs and brush, the ramada was the center of a Hohokam family's living area. Other features near their houses and ramadas included granaries, storage rooms, and roasting pits.

The Hohokam considered open space an important factor in village living. Each living area was separated from others by work spaces, cemeteries or unused, open desert. When a family grew too large for its area, part of the group established another residence some distance away. Sometimes families would abandon one area to allow a long-lived-in, dirty space to become clean again through exposure to the elements. After a time, the Hohokam sometimes reinhabited the abandoned areas of the village.

Within a given village, the people were probably all related to one another. They shared working spaces and cemetery plots between their living areas. A leader may have organized the settlement into work forces to tend irrigation ditches and harvest crops. Individuals got together for hunting and gathering expeditions.

We can imagine how the Hohokam from different villages socialized. People often met for informal talk or barter. Members from several settlements may have traveled together on expeditions to the Hohokam heartland or the Gulf of California. Secular and religious leaders organized intervillage ceremonies and celebrations. Some of the ceremonies revolved around ball courts. Villagers traveled from all over the basin to visit the villages along the Santa Cruz River that had ball courts. No one village or group of villages seemed to dominate others in the Tucson Basin.

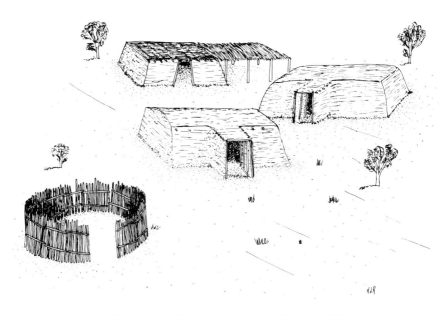

One or two families shared village space. In back of the two pit houses is a storeroom and attached ramada. A sheltered work area is at the lower left.

Hohokam Trade

A common Hohokam design painted on pottery depicts a walking figure with a hiking staff, carrying a bundle on his back. This figure is often referred to as the "burden basket carrier" and may be a trader. Since earliest times, the Hohokam were active traders. They received goods from western New Mexico, most of Arizona, and the coasts of California and Mexico, as well as from the more advanced cultures of west-central Mexico.

The Hohokam placed a high value on shell jewelry. We can imagine a trading trip to the Gulf of California or the California coast to procure unworked shell. A trading party would reach the gulf after walking more than 150 miles, carrying pottery, cloth, and other products to barter for shells. Indians living along the Gulf Coast probably met them to trade shells collected from the gulf throughout the year, in anticipation of the traders' arrival. Some of the shells, gathered from living shellfish, were much valued by the Hohokam for their color. After bartering with the Gulf Coast dwellers, the traders also gathered bleached and polished shells from the beaches. Experienced members of the party probably instructed those on their first expedition on how to select the proper shells to make pendants, bracelets, and beads. But the traders may not have always traveled to the coasts to collect shell. Some trade probably took place between the Hohokam and "middle men" who belonged to other cultural groups to the south and west of Hohokam territory.

Except for shell trade, the Hohokam's most important contact was with west-central Mexico, the probable origin of the Hohokam culture. Copper bells, polished plaques of iron pyrite, parrots, and macaws were obtainable there. Parrots and macaws were traded live into the Hohokam area, and the Indians probably used the birds' bright feathers in ceremonies. Copper bells, which resemble small sleigh bells, were sewn onto kilts or other clothing, or strung with beads to make necklaces, bracelets, and anklets. Iron pyrite plaques were stone discs, covered on one side with a mosaic of iron pyrite pieces. As with macaws, parrots, and copper bells, the plaques were probably used in ceremonies.

Stones prized for jewelry were also traded to the Hohokam. Among the stones traded were turquoise, serpentine, and argillite. Argillite and serpentine came from the Mogollon Rim region of Arizona. Turquoise may have come from southeastern Arizona or as far away as the Mohave Basin in California.

In addition to the other trade goods, the Tucson Basin Hohokam received pottery from the Hohokam heartland, the Mogollon people of Arizona and New Mexico, and the people of northern Sonora. Occasionally a pottery piece was brought in from western Mexico. We do not really know what the Hohokam traded in exchange for these goods. They may have traded finished jewelry, pottery, woven cotton fabrics, and food.

Ritual and Ceremony

The Hohokam had a rich ceremonial life, incorporating many ideas imported from Mesoamerica. In Mesoamerica a ball game played in depressed, rock-lined courts had ritual significance. This ball game and accompanying ritual spread north and was adopted by the Hohokam. They built oblong courts, usually large, mud plastered depressions resembling small football fields, to accommodate their version of the sport. The first Hohokam ball courts were built by A.D. 700. To honor ball players, Hohokam artisans sometimes made figurines with small shield pads on shin or shoulder.

At the same time that ball courts were introduced, platform mounds similar to those in Mesoamerica were built in the Hohokam heartland. These mounds were used in large rituals or celebrations that may have included dancing, since dancers were frequently painted on pottery vessels. Villagers participating in rituals wore elaborate headdresses, probably made of feathers, and may have painted their bodies with yellow, red, and purple mineral pigments and charcoal.

Cremation of the dead was widely practiced and probably involved ritualized activities. After a person died, the body was dressed, adorned with jewelry, and perhaps purified with incense. A crematory pit was filled with wood and a platform was built on top. After the body was laid on the platform, wood was piled on top of it and the whole thing was ignited. When the fire reached its highest point, a stone palette may have been placed on the pyre. A lead carbonate previously ground onto the palette would oxidize, creating a display of color.

When the fire died down, the remaining fragments of bone were gathered together and placed into a pottery vessel. The vessel was taken to a village cemetery and set in a pit. Personal possessions were

Macaws, small copper bells, and mosaic plaques made of iron pyrite were brought to the Hohokam from Mexico. All were probably used in ceremonies. Copper bells were often strung on necklaces with stone beads.

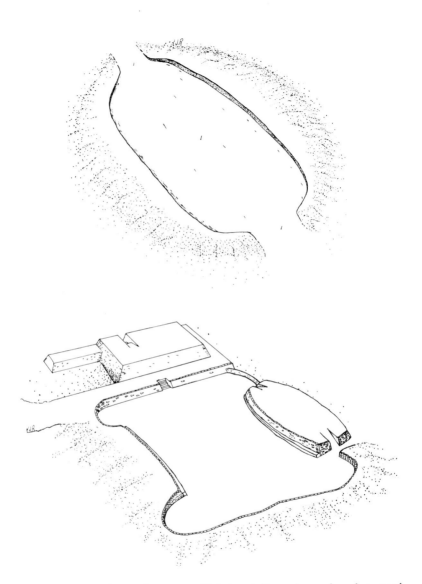

The structure at the top, known as a Hohokam ball court, may have been used to play a kick-ball type of game. The idea of building ball courts probably came from Mexico. The court at the bottom is at the site of Casas Grandes in Chihuahua, Mexico. (Casas Grandes court redrawn from DiPeso 1974.)

put with the vessel, and ceremonial objects, such as burned, broken palettes or figurines, were placed next to or in the pit, perhaps as a blessing. Finally, the pit was filled with earth. Ritual objects such as incense burners, pyrite plaques, figurines, and palettes were smashed and burned, and then left in caches at the cemetery. Relatives may have visited the cemetery periodically, to commemorate the dead.

The use of plaques, figurines, incense burners, and the tradition of sacrificing material objects with the dead were, like so many other Hohokam traits, Mesoamerican in origin. Incense burners were carved from stone or molded of clay. They were decorated with relief carvings of snakes, dancers, or horned lizards. Palettes varied in form from simple slabs of rock to ornately carved plates ornamented with snakes, birds, or horned lizards. The objects were usually made of slate or schist. Figurines made of fire-hardened clay occurred in many forms, but most were small, peg-legged objects with mask-like faces. Many were female and may have been fertility figures. Others may have been household gods or good-luck fetishes. Figurines of animals could have been hunting charms or toys.

Hohokam Influence on the Southwest

In 300 B.C., when the Hohokam moved north into Arizona from Mexico, the cultures of Mesoamerica were advanced in comparison with the hunters and gatherers then living in the Southwest. Consequently, the Hohokam brought with them some aspects of the higher civilizations of Mesoamerica. Because they maintained connections with Mesoamerican civilizations through the centuries, the Hohokam made social, religious, and artistic advances that were a bit ahead of their neighbors, the Patayan to the west, the Anasazi to the north, and the Mogollon to the east.

The Hohokam arrived in Arizona with the knowledge of pottery manufacture and canal irrigation. These technological skills enabled them to establish agricultural fields in the desert and store the produce of the fields during the winter. By A.D. 1200, the Hohokam had built hundreds of miles of canals in the Phoenix area alone.

Although Southwestern Indians had grown corn for a thousand years in the desert before the arrival of the Hohokam, they had never taken up full-time agriculture. The Hohokam dependence on farming gradually influenced some surrounding people to give up seminomadic hunting and gathering.

Mesoamerican contact before A.D. 1 inspired the Hohokam to develop techniques for carving shell and stone and for making turquoise mosaics. As a result of that inspiration, by A.D. 500, the Hohokam had become masters of ornate bone, stone, and shell carving. At first, the Mogollon and Anasazi found it easier to obtain shell and stone jewelry through Hohokam traders, but, later artisans of the two cultures began making jewelry on their own. The Anasazi mined their own turquoise and eventually produced the finest turquoise jewelry in the Southwest. They also became interested in other goods from Mexico, and, after trading through the Hohokam for a period of time, established trade directly with the civilizations of Mexico.

Clay human figurines, stone incense burners, and carved stone palettes were important in Hohokam ritual.

The Archaeological Record

The Hardy Site

One of the villages established by the Hohokam in the Tucson Basin lies southwest of the confluence of Pantano Wash and Rillito Creek. Known as the Hardy Site, the village today is beneath Fort Lowell Park and the surrounding neighborhood.

Hohokam people lived at the Hardy Site for almost a thousand years, from A.D. 300 to 1250. The earliest settlers at the village were probably colonists from the Gila-Salt River heartland. The Hardy Site is one of several early villages strategically located in the basin at points where farmland was abundant and natural resources were easily obtained.

The Hohokam at the Hardy Site farmed the rich bottomlands south of the Rillito and west of the Pantano. They crossed the Rillito to collect saguaro and other desert plants on the lower slopes of the Santa Catalina Mountains and ventured into the Catalinas to find pine and fir posts suitable for house and ramada buildings.

The Hardy Site villagers lived like their neighbors in the basin, changing gradually through time, but retaining their basic style of life. Then, around A.D. 1250, people began to abandon the Hardy Site village. The abandonment was not sudden. We imagine that a few families left at a time, moving to other villages near the Rillito River. As they left, the villagers scavenged valuable items from their houses. They pulled the large roof and wall supports from their homes and carried portable objects to the new villages. Over a period of years, the settlement was emptied.

Climate change at this time may have affected the subsistence patterns of the Indians, forcing them to concentrate on native plant foods

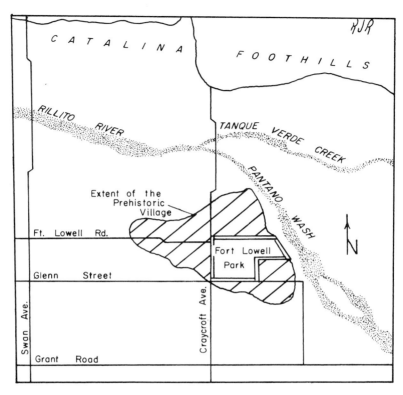

The Hardy Site is located just south of the confluence of Pantano Wash and Rillito Creek.

or to find new areas for farming. Undoubtedly, a combination of cultural and natural factors caused the abandonment of the Hardy Site and others in the basin, followed by the establishment of new villages.

Since the Hohokam abandoned the Hardy village, natural and human forces have changed its appearance. Houses and ramadas that were not dismantled collapsed shortly after the villagers left. Dust and dirt, carried in by wind and rain, gradually covered the houses, work areas, cemeteries, and trash mounds. Rabbits and ground squirrels burrowed into the soft powdery soil that blanketed the site. Bushes and weeds encroached on fields and living areas. A hundred years after its abandonment, only low mounds, patches of gray, ashy soil, and scattered debris marked the site.

The next human occupation of the site occurred in 1873, when the United States Army built Fort Lowell in the center of the prehistoric village. No known record details what Hohokam artifacts or features the builders of the fort found during construction. However, prehistoric debris must have been plentiful, since many of the fort adobes contain stone tools and pottery sherds. With the abandonment of the fort in 1891 came more construction and disturbance of the site. Houses, apartments, and other facilities built since that time have disturbed over seventy percent of the prehistoric village. The remaining, undamaged parts of the site are indicated by the presence of such cultural debris as sherds, pieces of bone and shell, and discarded stone tools.

Archaeological Survey

Many Hohokam sites in the Tucson Basin resemble the Hardy Site village. Amidst the modern buildings and debris of Tucson, low mounds and ancient trash are all that is left to indicate a Hohokam village, but even the most disturbed sites can yield a certain amount of information. For instance, one can tell the general age of a site by the types of pottery found. The type of site (for example, village or campsite) can also be determined sometimes. Campsites are small, often less than five acres, and contain very little decorated pottery. Villages, on the other hand, are larger, ranging in size from 5 to 200 acres, and there is decorated pottery in abundance. Low mounds covered with cultural debris are also often present at village sites.

Once an archaeologist determines the size and age of the sites in a given area, he can study the settlement pattern apparent from those sites. A settlement pattern study shows how a people used the topographic features of the region where they lived. For example, the Tucson Basin Hohokam built large villages on or just above the floodplain along the major streams in the basin. The large villages were situated near extensive tracts of arable land. Small, outlying villages, probably related to the larger villages, occurred on ridges at the junctions of mountain slopes and river terraces. The smaller villages were apparently located in areas suitable for hill-slope dry farming and collection of desert resources. The Hohokam also established campsites on lower mountain slopes, for the collection of foothill and mountain foods. Finally, the Indians used large exposures of rock in the foothills to carve pictures (petroglyphs); they created shrines in the higher mountains. Thus the Hohokam made use of almost every feature of the Tucson Basin.

Archaeological Excavation

Although generalizations can be made about the Hohokam from studying the remains on the ground surface at archaeological sites, more detailed information can be obtained only by excavation. (Much of what archaeologists know about peoples who lived in the past has been learned through excavation.) It has become possible to determine the differences between Hohokam villages and campsites by excavating several of each type of site. Relative ages of certain types of pottery are suggested by their placement in stratigraphic levels and by changes in designs, but exact ages for pottery and other artifacts can only be determined by tree-ring dates or comparisons with trade sherds from tree-ring dated sites.

There are many different ways to excavate a site. At the Hardy village, archaeologists selected three different techniques. First, they dug trenches to determine types and extent of subsurface remains (houses, trash pits, ramadas). Then, test pits, one by two meters (three by six feet) in size, were excavated into two trash mounds, to examine the time depth of each mound and the variety of trash discarded by the Hohokam. Finally, archaeologists laid out a grid system over a previously trenched area that promised undisturbed remains. They dug in squares of two by two meters, stripping areas down in ten centimeter (four inch) layers. An area totaling twenty by twenty meters (sixty by sixty feet) was stripped to the caliche level underlying the site.

Archaeologists mapped and photographed features such as pit houses and trash pits. Excavators labeled all artifacts (bone, shell, stone, and pottery) according to the grid square and layer in which they were found. The location of any artifact found within a feature was specifically recorded. For example, a metate resting on an ashy layer would be measured according to the grid square in which it was found, its exact horizontal location in the square, and its precise vertical depth below the ground surface. Archaeologists recorded in notebooks all of the information regarding locations of features and artifacts and saved the data for later study.

Regardless of the excavation technique used, the most important aspect in digging is recording the relationship between features and artifacts. A jar plucked out of the ground without regard to its location is of little value except for aesthetic considerations. A jar found in place on the floor of a burned house, on the other hand, is very useful in the interpretation of past events. By noting the jar in its place on the floor, an archaeologist might be able to determine whether the jar was used for storage or cooking. Contents of the vessel can be analyzed to determine what type of food or other material was inside at the time the house burned. If the jar was decorated, the age of the house could be determined.

In order to determine which structures and which objects were used at the same time, special care must be taken to assess the exact relationship between architectural features and artifacts. This is because most Hohokam villages were used continually over a long period of time. After houses were abandoned or destroyed, others were built on top of them. The Indians also used houses as trash repositories, or dug storage and cooking pits down into old houses and work areas. Features and artifacts thus become jumbled together and present a confusing picture to the archaeologist.

Archaeological Interpretation

After finishing an excavation and making all observations possible in the field, archaeologists then examine the material recovered in the course of the excavation. Pottery sherds are sorted according to type; broken vessels are mended; and the distribution of all pottery is examined. Stone tools are classified by possible use. A study of their distribution can show where in the village stone tools were made and where they were used. Recovery of small items like shell beads or figurines might indicate where a Hohokam broke a favorite necklace or lost a special talisman.

Geologists and biologists also aid in the analysis of recovered information and materials. Geologists establish the age of features at the site, using radiocarbon and archaeomagnetic dating methods. Another important dating method in the Southwest is tree-ring dating. Biologists identify animal bone and vegetal remains to determine what plants and animals the Hohokam used.

Because the data recovered from any excavation are fragmentary, a reconstruction based on the remains from one site is incomplete.

An excavated portion of the Hardy Site village is shown. The Hohokam continually reused portions of their villages over hundreds of years. Six pit houses an offertory area or cemetery, and a storage pit are visible in this photograph. The most recent houses, dating between A.D. 1100 and 1200, are in the left foreground and right background. Between them is the smooth, plastered, offertory area that was used from A.D. 500 to 700. In the center foreground, under the most recent house, is the earliest house at the site, which dates between A.D. 300 and 500.

Comparisons must be made with other excavations in an area. In order to reconstruct the Hardy village, it was compared to several other village sites in the Tucson Basin, including the Hodges Site, Punta de Agua sites, and University Indian ruin. Since the Hardy village is an open site, few remains of clothing and other perishable artifacts still existed. Ventana Cave, an excavated site on the Papago Reservation west of Tucson, provided most of the information known about perishable Hohokam goods.

In reconstructing activities at a site, prehistorians also use ethnographic information, that is, information about living people native to the region who are related to past residents. In southern Arizona, the

Pima and Papago way of life can be studied to better understand the way of life of the Hohokam. Most useful to the archaeologist is ethnographic information about behavior, such as the number of people living in one house, the reasons villages are arranged in certain ways, and the use of particular tools. The material evidence left by recorded ethnographic behavior is carefully observed. By comparing the ethnographic evidence with prehistoric remains, archaeologists can reconstruct the behavior of a prehistoric people.

Interpretation of the Hardy Site

In developing a picture of the Hardy village as it was a thousand years ago, we used both archaeological and ethnographic information. Only a tiny portion of the whole village was excavated. That part of the village was used at various times as a cemetery and housing area. Many pieces of evidence helped us reconstruct the history of this small part of the village.

In some cases, fate acting in the favor of the archaeologist provides evidence that would otherwise be lost. Basketry, sandals, and other objects made of vegetal materials rarely survive in open Hohokam sites. Occasionally burning will transform such objects into a more durable substance that resists the chemical erosion of desert soils. For example, if a basket is accidentally burned, it will survive a long time. Several pieces of charred basketry have been recovered from the Tucson Basin.

At the Hardy Site, no basketry was found. However, a clay stopper from a basketry vessel had been baked when a pit house burned, and was recovered. The stopper was originally a piece of soft clay that had been pressed over the opening of a rimless basket. In the fire, the basket completely burned away, but the basket's impression was left in the clay. Consequently, we have evidence of the original basket, its stopper, and a method of ancient storage.

In another burned house, the clay lining of the walls and posts was preserved. This baked-clay lining preserved impressions of reeds that also lined the walls. As with the basket stopper, soft clay was pressed against the reeds which formed the inner part of the wall. The reeds burned away leaving their fossil-like impressions on the hardened clay. From the floor of that house, an unusual fragment of clay with corncob impressions was also found. Evidently, the corn cobs were used as packing around an upright wall support, to make the post footing more solid. The clay was pressed around the corn cobs to create a smooth finish. The corncobs were burned out in the fire, but the packed clay, acting as a mold, retained the shape of the cobs around which it had been packed.

Burning preserved many vegetal remains in the form of charcoal. Charred remnants of juniper and Douglas fir posts were found in houses at the Hardy Site. The nearest source of such trees is in the Santa Catalina Mountains. The Hardy Site villagers must have trekked into the mountains to collect posts for their houses. Burned mesquite wood, saguaro ribs, and reeds found at the site provided information about Hohokam use of other parts of the basin.

Contact with other areas of the Southwest is indicated by trade goods discovered during excavation. The Hardy Site villagers apparently lost or threw away pieces of shell, turquoise, and other stones. One item, a large serpentine bead, was carefully shaped from a stone found along the Salt River, in central Arizona north of Globe (see page 14). It was found in an offertory cache and must have been highly valued by its owner.

Pottery was also traded into the village. Differences in painted design helped us to determine where the original pots were made. Most of the traded pottery came from the Hohokam heartland. This pottery is a red-on-buff ware. Its light color and porous texture show that it is from outside the basin.

The second largest group of trade pottery sherds are from bowls made in the Dragoon Mountains and the San Simon River valley in southeastern Arizona. These bowls were made by the Mogollon people and can be identified by their red exteriors and polished red-on-brown or red-on-white interiors.

Small amounts of pottery with black, polished interiors and sometimes textured exteriors were found. These sherds were from the extreme southeastern portion of Arizona and southwestern portion of New Mexico. The most obvious trade pottery found at the site were black-on-white sherds from the Mimbres Valley of New Mexico and the White Mountains of Arizona. These sherds, which came from the farthest distance, make up the smallest portion of trade pottery.

Events of daily life of the Hardy Site villagers could be assembled from data gathered during excavation. Around A.D. 1150, the people living in the excavated area made a working space adjacent to their house. The working space may have been shaded by a ramada. There, an archaeologist discovered two hammer stones used for chipping

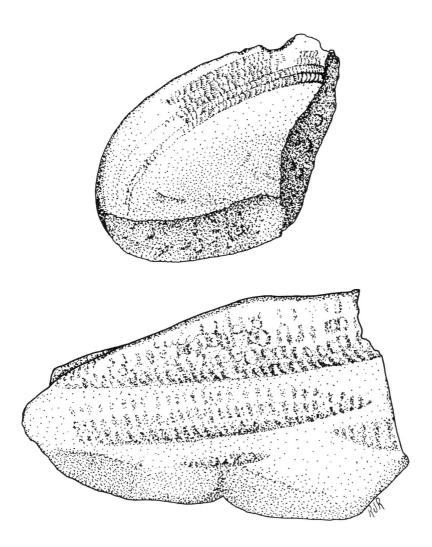

These burned adobe impressions of basketry (top) and corn cobs (bottom) were found in burned pit houses at the Hardy Site village.

stone tools, a pestle used for pounding seeds, a stone abrader used to smooth edges of shell, bone, or stone artifacts, a turquoise bead, and a tiny shell bead. The tools were not broken discards but had been left in place ready to be used again. The two small beads might have been lost while the Hohokam worked in the area.

Near the working space and house was a small room. Used for storage and cooking, the room burned down between A.D. 1125 and 1200. The fire must have consumed the room quickly, for several pottery vessels, manos, pestles, and a metate were left inside. Most of the pottery vessels were decorated and formed a cooking kit. Pieces included a storage jar, two small cooking jars, a bowl used for cooking, two small and one large mixing or serving bowls, one pouring bowl, a platter, and large sherds used as plates. All of the artifacts were found in one half of the house, as if the inhabitants had cleared the rest of the house for working space. That the room had been remodeled from an earlier house was shown by a second hearth underneath the plastered storeroom floor.

The ceramic vessels in this Hohokam "cooking kit" were found in a small storeroom at the site. Foods used by the Hohokam, in addition to corn, are —from left to right —barrel cactus fruit, tepary beans, saguaro seeds and cholla buds. All foods shown are modern examples.

Underneath several house floors, there was a compressed layer of ash barely one centimeter thick. As the digging progressed, patches of a plastered surface and small pits filled with burned human bone were uncovered beneath the ash layer. Near the center of the plastered surface was a large pottery bowl painted with floral designs. The bowl's exterior was incised and decorated with parallel lines. The technique of decoration indicates that the bowl was made between A.D. 500 and 700. Next to the bowl there was a small pottery incense burner painted red and also incised. It once had four small legs that were broken off before the vessel was placed on the surface. Both of the pottery vessels were placed on the surface upside down.

The next find was a small, fired, female figurine, made of clay. Its body was realistically modeled from two coils of clay. The face of the figurine was mask-like, rectangular with incised slit eyes and a pinched-up nose. The find of a whole figurine is rare in the Hohokam area, because the Indians usually broke figurines before placing them with a cremation.

We were able to determine from these objects the ritual nature of the ash-covered surface. Other offerings and the small amounts of human bone indicated that the surface was an offertory area or cemetery. The artifacts on it were blessings left to commemorate the dead, when the surface was in use between A.D. 500 and 700.

As these and other fragments of evidence were assembled, the history of part of the Hardy Site village was revealed. When the village began around A.D. 300, at least one family lived in the excavated area, but, by A.D. 500, the use of the area had changed. At first, the Hohokam dug pits from which they mined caliche for use in plaster and adobe. Later, they filled the pits with trash. Adjacent to those pits, the Indians established a cemetery and plastered offertory area. The area, used from A.D. 500 to 700, was plastered and may have had a ramada-like shade over it.

Shortly thereafter, one or two families again built houses in the area, but did not remain very long. From A.D. 800 to around 1000, the Hohokam used the excavated area infrequently as a work area or path. Then, around A.D. 1000, one or two families again built houses in the area, digging through the earlier cemetery and houses in the process. In A.D. 1100, two new, adobe-walled, pit houses were built, and villagers remodeled an older pit house and used it as a storage room until it caught fire and burned.

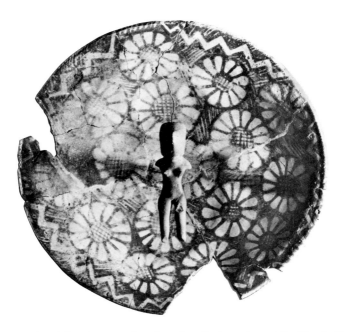

This bowl and figurine were found on the offertory plaza at the Hardy Site village. They date between A.D. 500 and 700 and were probably traded into the area from the Gila and Salt River valleys. The flower design on the bowl is rare.

At around A.D. 1200, the houses in the excavated area were abandoned. They lay empty for several years but were reused briefly after the village was finally abandoned in A.D. 1250. The nature of the reuse is unknown, but may have been nothing more than the result of children at play.

The Hardy Site is only one example of an excavated Hohokam village, but by comparing the few other excavated sites with the Hardy village, a composite story of the Tucson Basin Hohokam has been developed. The story will never be complete because of natural and human factors that have changed the sites through time. However, the history of the Hohokam that has emerged is one of a people who were able to adapt to a desert environment by combining agriculture with hunting and gathering. The Hohokam developed a unique culture that lasted for over a thousand years in the Sonoran Desert.

Glossary

Agave (*Agave* sp.)—sometimes called a century plant. Several species of the plant were used by Indians in the Southwest and Mexico. The plants vary greatly in size, but are characterized by a cluster of leaves spreading out at ground level from a short central stem. The narrow leaves are long and thick and terminate in a spine. At maturity, each plant sends up one long flowering stalk and then dies. Agaves grow at elevations of 3000 to 8000 feet. Species of agave are used in the manufacture of pulque and tequila, alcoholic beverages popular in Mexico. Raw agave is poisonous.

Anasazi—the prehistoric peoples who occupied parts of a region extending from southwestern Nevada on the west to the edge of the Great Plains in New Mexico and Colorado on the east, and from northeastern Utah and northwestern Colorado on the north, to central New Mexico and the Little Colorado River in Arizona on the south. Remains of the Anasazi culture include the ruins at Chaco Canyon, Mesa Verde, Canyon de Chelly, and the Navajo National Monument. Like the Hohokam, the Anasazi developed out of an Archaic tradition to become sedentary farmers. The Anasazi lifeway first emerged around the time of Christ. The first Anasazi are known as Basketmakers. The lifeway continues today in the New Mexican pueblos and Hopi villages.

Archaeomagnetic dating—a method of dating based on the wandering of the earth's magnetic north pole. When the clay-lined hearths used by the Hohokam were heated, minute magnetic particles in the clays realigned themselves with magnetic north. Through a process that involves careful testing of collected samples of hearths with a magnetometer, the date of a given hearth can be determined.

Argillite—fine-grained, metamorphosed mud and claystone. The deep-red-colored argillite artifacts found at the Hardy Site may have come from the Mazatzal Mountains in central Arizona.

Arrow weed (*Pluchea servicea*)—a rank-smelling shrub that forms dense thickets in stream beds and moist saline soil. The plant occurs at elevations of 3000 feet or lower, from Texas to southern California and from Utah to northern Mexico. In addition to its use as a wall-covering material, arrow weed stems were used for arrow shafts by Indians in the Southwest.

Basin and Range Province—a geographic area extending from southern Oregon and Idaho to northern Mexico, and including most of western Arizona, the Great Basin of Utah and Nevada, and parts of eastern California. It is an area characterized by north-south trending mountain ranges interspersed by flat basins. The area was formed initially through block faulting during Tertiary times (15–20 million years ago), when, in a series of earthquakes, one section of land was lifted while the adjacent portion was lowered.

Bear grass *(Nolina microcarpa)*—also called sacahuista. Resembling clumps of large, coarse grass, this plant is found on mountain slopes around the Tucson Basin at elevations of 3000 to 6000 feet.

Caliche—deposits of calcium carbonate that occur as the substrata throughout much of the Tucson Basin. Caliche occurs as irregular, impervious layers a fraction of an inch to several feet in thickness, or as the matrix in a sand and gravel conglomerate. The formation of caliche is an ongoing process. Many of the pottery sherds and pieces of stone tools found at the Hardy Site were covered with caliche.

Cholla *(Opuntia sp.)*—several species of spiny cactus having cylindrical stems and branches. The plants are found in many parts of semiarid and arid North America.

Desert Archaic Tradition—a seminomadic, hunting and gathering way of life that people in the Southwest adopted around 7000 B.C. The tradition is also known in Arizona as the Cochise, Amargosan, or Desert culture. The Desert Archaic lifeway was widespread, extending into the Great Basin of Utah and Nevada and the Mohave Desert of California. Although the Archaic lifeway gradually disappeared in southern Arizona as the Hohokam culture developed, the tradition was practiced into historic times by people such as the Great Basin Paiute.

Devil's claw *(Martynia parviflora or Proboscidea parviflora)*—also called the unicorn plant. A coarse, low-growing annual with large, shallowly lobed leaves. All parts of the plant are covered with coarse, sticky hairs. The seedpods turn black at maturity and each is characterized by a long, slightly curved extension of its tip. The plants grows at elevations of 1000 to 5000 feet and ranges from western Texas to southern Nevada.

Douglas fir *(Pseudotsuga taxifolia)*—a tall evergreen found at elevations of 6500 to 10,000 feet. Used by the Hohokam for timber, this tree can be found in the higher mountain ranges surrounding the Tucson Basin.

Dry farming—method where rainfall runoff is diverted or trapped to provide water for crops. Dry-farming systems include terraces, check dams, and small ditches.

Ethnographic information—information obtained from the anthropological study of living peoples.

Gulf of California—also known as the Sea of Cortez, it is the body of water separating Baja, California from the rest of Mexico. The Colorado River empties into the gulf.

Hematite—an important form of iron ore that is very widely distributed. Hematite occurs in many different forms. The powdered mineral is metallic to dull in luster, dull to bright red in color. One form of hematite that is found in the Tucson area is specular hematite, which has a metallic, purple color in crushed form.

Ice Age—also known as the Pleistocene Epoch, this is the geologic period of time when glaciers alternately advanced and retreated over much of North America and Eurasia. The length of the Pleistocene is still a matter of debate. It may extend from three million to nine thousand years ago. Arizona was never covered by glaciers. However, when glaciers advanced over the land, Arizona's climate became wetter and slightly cooler.

Iron pyrite—a metallic, yellow-to-brown sulfide of iron. This widely occurring mineral is also known as fool's gold. The mineral is cubic in crystal form.

Juniper *(Juniperus* sp.) —small to medium-sized evergreen trees with scaly leaves. Trunks and branches of the trees are often twisted. Various species grow at elevations of 3000 to 8000 feet in southern Arizona.

Kiln—a brick-lined oven used to fire ceramics.

Lac—a resinous deposit of an insect that lives on creosote bushes.

Limonite—a substance produced by the oxidation of iron-bearing minerals such as pyrite and magnetite. Limonite is a yellowish brown, soft mineral with no cleavage. It is a widely occurring mineral.

Macaw—large, brightly colored, tropical American birds closely resembling and related to parrots.

Mammoth—extinct relatives of the elephant that roamed North America and Eurasia during the Ice Age.

Manzanita *(Arctostaphylus* sp.) —also called bearberry. Manzanita is a low-growing evergreen shrub that is found at elevations of 3500 to 8000 feet. The plant is characterized by its red bark and oval-shaped leaves.

Mesoamerica—a geographical culture area extending from central Honduras and northwestern Costa Rica on the south, and, in Mexico, from the Río Soto la Marina in Tamaulipas and the Río Fuerte in Sinaloa on the north. Prehistoric groups in this area are characterized by agricultural villages and large ceremonial and politico-religious capitals. Well known cultural groups within Mesoamerica include Mayans, Aztecs, Olmecs, Mixtecs, Toltecs, and Zapotecs. The Chalchihuites culture of northwestern Mesoamerica probably had the most influence on the Hohokam.

Mesquite *(Prosopis* sp.)—a thorny plant that ranges from shrub to tree size. It grows at elevations below 5000 feet from southern Kansas to southwestern California and northern Mexico.

Mogollon—the prehistoric cultural groups who lived in an area which includes southern New Mexico, southeastern and central Arizona, the El Paso area in Texas, and northwestern Chihuahua Mexico. The Mogollon lifeway began about the same time the Hohokam entered southern Arizona. Although they grew crops, the Mogollon continued to make extensive use of native food resources. Around A.D. 1000, they became influenced by the Anasazi, another southwestern group. The Mogollon culture died out around A.D. 1450, and the people abandoned the Mogollon region, some perhaps merging with the Zuni.

Mohave Basin—the geographic area encompassing the Mohave Desert in California, north of the Imperial Valley and south of Death Valley.

Ocotillo *(Fouqueria splendens)*—this plant, also called the coach whip, is characterized by clumps of straight, thorny whip-like stems with no branches. When there is adequate rainfall, the ocotillo leafs out, but loses its leaves when the soil dries. The plant has brilliant red flowers that occur at the tips of its many stems. Ocotillos occur below 5000 feet, from west Texas to southeastern California and northern Mexico.

Paleo-Indian Tradition (also called Big Game Hunting Tradition)—a way of life practiced by many of the first human inhabitants of North America, who arrived here between 10,000 and 12,000 years ago. Paleo-Indian means the oldest or first Indians in North America. In Arizona, Paleo-Indians hunted with spears tipped with Clovis points. Two important Paleo-Indian sites in Arizona are the Naco and Lehner sites in the southeastern part of the state.

Patayan—the prehistoric cultural groups that occupied the region west of the Hohokam culture area. The boundaries of the Patayan area are, on the west, the Colorado River Delta north to above Needles, and, on the east, from Gila Bend to Prescott. The Patayan practiced a lifeway similar to the Hohokam, although hunting and gathering were more emphasized in the Patayan culture. The Patayan were probably ancestral to the Yuma tribes that occupied the area historically. The culture is first recognized at A.D. 700.

Pigweed *(Amaranthus sp.)*—a common, coarse weed that grows in disturbed soil. It usually appears after summer rains at elevations below 5500 feet.

Piñon pine *(Pinus cembroides)*—a pine tree that grows at elevations of 5000 to 7500 feet. The piñon bears large edible nuts.

Ponderosa pine *(Pinus ponderosa)*—also called the yellow pine. This large tree grows at elevations of 5500 to 8500 feet.

Prickly pear *(Opuntia sp.)*—several species of cacti with flat stems and oval, flat, leaf-like pads. Prickly pears grow in semiarid and arid western North America. The fruits of the cactus are often referred to as "tunas."

Radiocarbon dating—also called Carbon-14 dating, the method measures the amount of radioactive carbon contained in a sample of organic material. All living organisms absorb a form of carbon dioxide that contains Carbon 14. When the organism dies, the radioactive carbon begins to change back to its original structure. The rate of change can be measured. Carbon 14 has a half-life of about 5700 years, meaning that, after that amount of time, the organism retains one-half the amount of Carbon 14 it had immediately after death. The radiocarbon dating method has been used throughout the world to date archaeological remains.

Ramada—an open-air shade built of upright posts that are covered with a flat roof. The Pimas and Papagos also made use of the ramada as a focal point of family activity.

Ranchería—a form of village arrangement in which individual dwellings are widely separated. This can be contrasted with the Pueblo style of architecture in which dwellings within a village are attached to one another in an apartment-like complex.

44

Saguaro *(Cereus gigantea)* — one of the largest cacti, the saguaro has one central trunk with one or more upward curving branches. This tree-size cactus played an important role in the economy of the Hohokam and the Pima and Papago cultures.

Serpentine — a metamorphic mineral altered from limestone or basic igneous rocks such as olivine and amphibole. One form of serpentine — chrysolite — is a common source of asbestos.

Sonoran Desert — a region stretching from Parker, Wickenburg, and the Tonto Basin in Arizona on the north; to the Río Culiacán in Sinaloa, Mexico on the south; east to the Sierra Madre Occidental in Mexico, and the Huachuca, Santa Catalina, Rincon, and Pinaleño Mountains in Arizona; and west to the Gulf of California, the Colorado River delta, and the Salton Sea in California. The desert includes parts of the state of Sinaloa, most of Sonora, and the northeast corner of Baja California in Mexico; and the southern half of Arizona and the southeastern corner of California in the United States. The area is characterized by vegetation ranging from creosote bush and bursage at lower elevations to palo verde, mesquite, and saguaro at higher elevations.

Steatite — a soft, easily worked stone found in many localities in Arizona. The rock is a form of talc and is commonly associated with serpentine.

Tansy mustard *(Descurainia* sp.*)* — annual plants that grow in open soil. Tansy mustard has small, yellow flowers and blooms in early spring.

Tree-ring dating — also known as dendrochronology, it is a dating method based on the sequence of annual growth rings in trees. Dendrochronologists have charted the differences in ring width from year to year (widths are affected by annual rainfall). By overlapping the growth sequence chart from live and recently cut trees to trees cut by prehistoric people, scientists have built chronologies for various areas extending back over a thousand years. Thus, a beam taken from a ruin can often be dated by matching its growth sequence to the chronology. Chronologies have not yet been established for the Hohokam area.

Water table — the level of groundwater below which all cavities are filled and permeable rock formations are saturated with water. In the Tucson Basin, the water table, or groundwater level, is added to by gentle winter rains which soak into the ground and eventually find their way into the underground reservoir.

Yucca *(Yucca* sp.*)* — several plants that are members of the lily family. The plants grow throughout the Southwest at elevations of 1500 to 6000 feet. Plants are characterized by a clump of thin, pointed leaves at the base and a single flowering stalk. White flowers appear on the stalks each spring. The plant is important not only for its fiber but for soap obtained from the root and for the use of its seeds, fruits, and flowers as food.

Bibliography

From the list of references used in the preparation of this booklet, there are several of interest to those wishing to obtain more information on the Tucson Basin, the Hohokam, and the Pima and Papago. Hastings and Turner's *The Changing Mile* and Dunbier's *The Sonoran Desert* contain facts about the Tucson Basin, the Sonoran Desert, and people's changing use of the desert. For anyone wanting to know more about the Hohokam, the two books by Haury, *The Hohokam: Desert Farmers and Craftsmen* and *The Stratigraphy and Archaeology of Ventana Cave,* are essential. To those books, *Excavations at Snaketown: Material Culture* by Gladwin, Haury, Sayles, and Gladwin should be added. Snaketown, examined by both Haury and Gladwin, was a large Hohokam community on what is now the Gila River Indian Reservation. Many of our current ideas about the Hohokam come from the excavation and interpretation of this village. Those interested in Tucson Basin archaeology should read Greenleaf's *Excavations at Punta de Agua* and Kelly's *The Hodges Ruin.* Recommended readings about the Pima and Papago are Castetter and Bell's *Pima and Papago Indian Agriculture,* Russell's *The Pima Indians,* which was reprinted in 1975 by The University of Arizona Press, Shaw's *A Pima Past,* and Webb's *A Pima Remembers.*

References

Bancroft, Hubert H.
   1883   *The Works of Hubert Howe Bancroft Vol. 1 The Native Races: 1 Wild Tribes.* A. L. Bancroft and Company, San Francisco.
Bartlett, John Russell
   1854   *Personal Narative of the Explorations and Incidents in Texas, New Mexico, California, Sonora, and Chihuahua.* Vols. 1 and 2, D. Appleton and Company, New York.
Castetter, E. F. and W. H. Bell
   1942   Pima and Papago Indian Agriculture. *Inter-Americana Studies* No. 1, University of New Mexico Press, Albuquerque.

Castetter, E. F. and R. Underhill
  1935   The Ethnobiology of the Papago Indians. *University of New Mexico Bulletin, Biology Series* Vol. 4, No. 3.
Dunbier, Roger
  1968   *The Sonoran Desert.* University of Arizona Press, Tucson.
Gladwin, Harold S., Emil W. Haury, E. B. Sayles, Nora Gladwin
  1965   *Excavations at Snaketown, Material Culture.* Reprint edition. University of Arizona Press, Tucson.
Greenleaf, J. Cameron
  1975   Excavations at Punta de Agua. *Anthropological Papers of the University of Arizona* No. 26.
Hastings, James R. and Raymond M. Turner
  1965   *The Changing Mile.* University of Arizona Press, Tucson.
Haury, Emil W.
  1950   *The Stratigraphy and Archaeology of Ventana Cave, Arizona.* University of New Mexico Press, Albuquerque, and University of Arizona Press, Tucson.
  1976   *The Hohokam: Desert Farmers and Craftsmen.* University of Arizona Press, Tucson.
Haynes, C. Vance
  1966   Elephant Hunting in North America. *Scientific American* Vol. 214, No. 6, pp. 104–112.
Johnson, Alfred E.
  1960   The Place of the Trincheras Culture of Northern Sonora in Southwestern Archaeology. MS, Master's Thesis, University of Arizona.
Kelly, Isabel T.
  1978   The Hodges Ruin: A Hohokam Community in the Tucson Basin. *Anthropological Papers of the University of Arizona* No. 30.
Russell, Frank
  1908   The Pima Indians. *Twenty-Sixth Annual Report of the Bureau of American Ethnology.*
Sayles, E. B. and Ernst Antevs
  1941   The Cochise Culture. *Medallion Papers* No. 29. Gila Pueblo, Globe, Arizona.
Sellers, William D. and R. H. Hill
  1974   *Arizona Climate: 1931–1972.* University of Arizona Press, Tucson.
Shaw, Anna Moore
  1974   *A Pima Past.* University of Arizona Press, Tucson.
Smith, G. E. D.
  1910   Groundwater Supply and Irrigation in the Rillito Valley. *Arizona Agricultural Experiment Station Bulletin* No. 64.
Tanner, Clara Lee
  1976   *Prehistoric Southwestern Craft Arts.* University of Arizona Press, Tucson.
Underhill, Ruth
  1939   *Social Organization of the Papago Indians.* Columbia University Press, New York.
Webb, George
  1959   *A Pima Remembers.* University of Arizona Press, Tucson.
Willey, Gordon
  1966   *An Introduction to American Archaeology. Vol 1: North and Middle America.* Prentice-Hall, Englewood Cliffs, New Jersey.